MOBILE HOME

TYCOON

Cash Flow & Big Profits

MOBILE HOME

TYCOON

Cash Flow & Big Profits

RJ Salerno

For information, visit www.rjsalerno.com

Book and Cover design by RJ Salerno

MOBILE HOME TYCOON: Cash Flow & Big Profits

ISBN: 978-1676342724

First Edition: April 2018 - 10 9 8 7 6 5 4 3 2 1

TABLE OF CONTENTS

INTRODUCTION

This is an A to Z, beginners guide into the world of mobile home real estate investing and untapped opportunities unknown to the seasoned real estate investor. There are many valuable tips and examples to put you on your way to begin amassing your own real estate empire. I will walk you through on how to find your very 1st mobile home deal and on how to begin cash flowing immediately on your new investment.

Some years ago, I was introduced to the world of real estate investing. Like most that are in the investment world, there are many aspects of real estate investing I had to learn. Most investors that I knew stayed away from mobile homes. Mostly what I was told was of the pitfalls and investment failures when investing in mobile homes. Since then what I have found are a very small margin of real estate investors in this world of mobile home investing and they are making a fortune.

What this means to you is a huge opportunity to capitalize on a wide-open market. Most of what I have learned has been by trial and error since there are very few books or course on the matter. Two people (Lonnie Scruggs and Zalman Velvel) have been the pioneers in mobile home investing and have made their own success as real estate investors with mobile homes.

CHAPTER 1
INCREDIBLE INVESTMENT

Investing in a mobile home could be your most profitable investment outlet in today's market. In a suffering economy, finding a lucrative investment is essential. While real estate is generally thought to be a solid investment, there are not a lot of homes being purchased. In the present condition of our economy, more people are interested in renting a home than buying one. We will not only discuss the benefits of a mobile home investment; we will also take a look at some of the best practices for generating sufficient revenue from one or more mobile homes.

Why mobile home rentals? Get past the prejudice and look at the numbers. In our town, for example, a two bedroom house costs $130,000 and rents for $900/month. A $50,000 mobile home on real estate gets $600/month. Cash-on-cash return on investment is obviously higher with mobile homes.

Don't let the half-truth that mobiles depreciate in value keep you from investing in them. They lose value in a park, on a rented lot, but not on real estate. My first home was a mobile, bought for $39,000 and sold it for $58,000 five years later

House rentals here usually have negative cash flow, while mobile home rentals have some cash flow. Still, investors prefer houses, believing they'll build equity faster, but is that true? Only during times of fast appreciation.

EQUITY BUILDING WITH RENTALS

Buy a house for $120,000 with $20,000 down, and take out a $100,000, 6%, 30-year mortgage. You'll have a payment of $599.60. Of the first payment, $500 will go to interest, and $99.60 to principal. You only built equity of $99.60. This ignores appreciation, but only for the moment

Second scenario: Find a mobile home for sale on land, and borrow $30,000, at 8%, amortized over 10 years. Higher interest and a shorter term is normal with mobiles, but being done with payments in 10 years instead of 30 isn't all bad. The payment will be $363.99. The first month, $200 will go to interest, and $163.99 to principal. You built more equity in this scenario.

Mobile home rentals on land might appreciate more slowly than the "regular" house, but faster loan pay-down usually covers this factor. Pay less per month, have positive instead of negative cash flow, and build more equity! Don't expect your real estate agent to tell you this.

Cash Flow

In the example, you'd lose about $150/month on the house, after the payment, taxes, insurance, repairs and other expenses. You'd have cash flow with the mobile home, and after ten years (when the loan is paid off), you'd have a lot of cash flow.

Mobiles are cheap to maintain. The furnace died in rental I owned, and I replaced it for $1,200, much less than a furnace for a larger home. For $200, you can have the roof tarred, instead of $5,000 to re-shingle a traditional roof. Windows, plumbing, doors – they're all cheaper. Property taxes and insurance are less too (be sure you can get insurance, since some old mobiles may be uninsurable).

Bottom Line

$20,000 can buy two mobiles, with $10,000 down on each, or four with $5,000 down on each, instead of one negative-cash-flow house. The two investors in our town that own most of the mobile homes always have cash flow, and have built millions in equity. Others, following their prejudices, struggle to make money with their "nice" rental homes. So when you're looking for a good investment, don't forget those mobile home rentals.

CHAPTER 2
INVESTING IN MOBILE HOMES WITH LAND

The mobile home and land deal is a combination investment. Using any one of the techniques found in creative real estate investing, buying land with a mobile home on it, or buying a mobile home and place it on land you have purchased. The mobile home itself is initially treated as personal property, much like a car. The land is treated as real estate.

By combining the two, we create a land/home deal. This new package is typically worth much more than the two components individually. In other words, by combining the mobile home with the land, value is created.

Less Competition

You do not have to compete with all of those investors who advertise: "I Buy Ugly Houses." You do not have to compete with new investors who just purchased a *No Money Down* type course from some late night infomercial. Just as I was skeptical in the beginning, many others are, too.

Mobile home investors are comparably fewer and farther between.

Minimal Risk

What first attracted me to mobile home investing was the small amount of money needed to invest. In most cases what was found, I invested no more money when buying both the mobile home and the land than I did when I bought a mobile home on someone else's land.

With mortgage payments between $200 and $400 per deal, I was able to overcome the fear of someone not paying. Knowing that if all else failed; I could find some sort of work to make that kind of payment. Initially I would not have felt confident if the payment was the $700 to $900 per month that was found in traditional real estate investments.

Figured I could buy a doublewide mobile home and land for $40,000 and receive a minimum positive income of $200 per month (after all debt and expenses are paid). Why would I pay twice that much or more for an older, smaller, stick-built, single-family home that gave us the same $200 per month positive cash flow?

Appreciation

I have found that doublewide, land/home properties appreciate in a manner similar to comparable stick-built homes. Appreciation is viewed as a bonus and focus primarily on creating a positive cash flow and capturing equity through wholesale purchases.

Demand

By focusing on marketing and property acquisitions to address the needs of the lower to middle income housing market, I find that the demand for my properties remains high in both good and bad economies.

Typically, when times are good, more entry-level jobs are available, which means more people who need affordable housing. In poor economies, downsizing occurs. People are no longer able to afford to live above their means, forcing them to find affordable housing.

Less Expensive Maintenance

Not only are the land and home deals less expensive than traditional real estate investments, I find that the mobile home repairs are easier and less expensive. I try to provide the safest, cleanest property that can at each price level.

My properties all fall within the low to lower middle-income family range. These tenants cannot reasonably have the same quality expectations as families who pay more to live in stick-built homes of comparable size.

Often, an investor who is reasonably patient and minimally skilled can make the repairs--saving him the cost of hiring someone else to do it. If the investor does not wish to make the repairs himself, the job can be hired out to a handyman.

Investment Benefits

I prefer to rent my land/home properties. Each new property provides with a larger positive monthly cash flow. Each new property we gain is like receiving a raise at work.

Additionally, tax laws allow me to depreciate the properties and write off expenses. These paper losses offset our income, which means I legally get to keep more of our money and pay less in taxes.

Competitive Product

If a mobile home becomes outdated or the floor plan no longer appeals to the market, I can simply remove the mobile home and replace it with a newer home that meets consumer demands.

By purchasing used or repossessed mobile homes, I can make these upgrades very quickly and inexpensively. Try doing that with a stick-built, single-family home or apartment!

Greater Control

When I do not own the land, I am subject to the whims of the park manager or property owner who can always ask me to move the home. They are also able to choose the tenants who move into the park.

This can cost you time and money--some park managers are slow decision makers. They have little incentive to act quickly if they believe the investor will pay the lot rent each month.

By owning both the mobile home and the land, I become the landlord with the final say about my properties. When owning the land, I control the decision of to whom we rent and how long they stay. In addition, I have well-defined landlord/tenant laws to use should a tenant stop paying or breach the lease.

Typically, an eviction is easier and faster than repossession, most everyone in the process understands an eviction. Because mobile home repossessions are not done frequently, I found that a new sheriff's deputy, magistrate, or judge would often confuse the issues and create unnecessary delays and expenses for me.

Leverage

Leverage is the greatest advantage that land/home deals have over buying a mobile home in a park. Rather than invest money to buy an older mobile home in a park, that same money could be leveraged through loans to buy a land and home package.

This property becomes a long-term rental property providing the investor with a similar cash flow, but with added advantages of equity build up and tax savings through depreciation. In essence, I am controlling a much more valuable property with the same amount of money.

I have found that lenders are more comfortable with real estate investments than they are with mobile home note investments. Lenders can quickly confirm real estate values through appraisals, comparable sales, and tax assessments. It is suspected lenders naturally discount the value of mobile home notes when looking at the investor's net worth.

Ultimate Retirement Plan

The single most unique aspect of investing in mobile homes on land is the ability to sell the mobile home and rent the land. It is hard to imagine a more passive real estate investment than owning and renting only land. As Lonnie Scruggs says, "it is hard to hurt the dirt."

CHAPTER 3
SENIOR HOUSING IS INVESTING FOR A FUTURE

So what does that mean for you, real estate investors, landlords and other interested parties? Why, it means you need to know what seniors are looking for in their retirement living, of course! You have the perfect opportunity to put a shine on someone's golden years. While single seniors spring for both rental homes and apartments, we're going to look specifically at the best ways to attract and accommodate independent seniors looking to make the most of their retirement.

Baby Boomers are turning 65 and fewer and fewer seniors are moving into retirement communities. They're going to suburbs as much as cities. With such varied preferences, it's impossible to be perfect for every senior. That doesn't mean, however, that there aren't common threads and steps to be taken to attract and please the valuable and growing demographic of independent seniors — who, by the way, are often opting the sell their homes and rent instead for a lot of reasons: a lack of property taxes, fewer upkeep responsibilities and lease and travel flexibilities, just to name a few.

Independent seniors looking to rent a home or an apartment are looking for things that are a little different from the average tenant. Remember that not all tenants will need or want everything on this list — it's just a starting point to get you thinking about how to target the growing numbers of retirees looking for rental housing.

Retirement Living Keeping These In Mind
Retirees may not want to deal with the headache of mowing a lawn and pruning back the crepe myrtles, but that doesn't mean they want to be stuck without a way to enjoy the outdoors at their own home. Having a small, highly manageable yard is a huge plus for seniors (especially if yard maintenance is included in the rent) who want to enjoy being out in nature. An apartment complex that has outdoor walking paths and outdoor community areas with tables and chairs for socializing is also a big selling point.

Public Transportation

Keep in mind that your tenants may not drive as much as they used to, either by choice or by inability. A location with convenient access to buses, taxis and other public transportation means your tenants can get out on the town and enjoy all the amenities of your city. They may want to live it up while they still can!

Smaller Spaces

When it comes to retired tenants, a smaller square footage is your friend. Just like a smaller yard, a downsize in floor space means less to clean and manage. This isn't to say potential tenants want to be cramped in an apartment the size of a bread box, but they may not need or want the spaciousness of a nine room family home with three or four bedrooms. Think simple and stylish – go for the necessities but not too many extras.

Handicap Accessibility

Here's an addendum. Smaller doesn't mean cramped. Doorways need to be wide enough for the navigation of walkers, canes and wheelchairs.

Having more limited mobility is already a pain when the corners are easy to navigate, so don't make it harder for your seniors! Even if they are still independent, it doesn't mean they don't have special mobility that should be taken into account. Pay attention to the needs of individuals – they might require walk-in/roll-in showers, the installation of grab bars, lever door handles and even chair-level peep holes in the front door. While it's not necessary to make every unit in your complex handicap-accessible, having a few (near the roomy elevator that you also have, by the way) will come in handy. Remember, too, that under the Fair Housing Act, landlords must allow modifications to meet the needs of a handicapped individual, even if that means requiring the tenant to return the unit to its original state before moving.

Ground Level

If your housing isn't ground level, you need to have an elevator. Stairs aren't great for seniors, whether or not they have walkers, canes or wheelchairs. They're hard on the knees! Going up and down stairs can be hazardous, particularly for seniors. Don't put them at risk.

Fitness Facilities

Throw your preconceptions out the window. Today's seniors aren't sitting around watching Jeopardy all day. This is 2013, the age of the active senior! Providing a well-equipped gym and walking area is a great way to get seniors socializing with neighbors, get out of their apartments and live a more active, healthy lifestyle. In single-family housing, providing opportunities for seniors to be active is a huge plus and it may be advantageous to make deals with local gyms for your tenants to have memberships and roll it up into the rent. I may not go so far as to include any exercise equipment in one of the bedrooms, but I am sure some smart landlord will give it a try and make it work.

Emergency and Security Services

Because single seniors are likely living alone unless they have roommates, extra security precautions are important. Make sure you (or your property manager) pay special attention the safety of your senior tenants. If something happens, they need to be able to get in contact with someone who can help immediately. Don't ever let your tenants feel unsafe in their home. Check on things regularly with their safety in mind. While plenty of independent seniors don't want to be coddled or doted on, being attentive is part of being a good landlord. This is another area where a monitored security system can be provided by the owner/management and the monthly cost simply rolled into the rent.

No Retirement Community

Don't feel pressured to have dining services and healthcare or scheduled activities just because you're looking to have senior residents. Retirement living doesn't necessarily mean your complex has to turn into it's own self-sustained, full-equipped community with room service. What's important when it comes to seniors — as much as any potential tenant — is to listen and to respect their needs and desires in a property. Accommodate to the best of your ability and treat them like the valuable tenants that they are.

Obviously with single-family housing accommodated for senior living, you are not going to have meal services, but do not discount the value of making things easy. Really smart entrepreneurs are going to figure out how to cost effectively offer delivered meal services (already happening), security systems (already happening), electric, water and cable services provided (already happening) and even therapeutic services on location (already happening). When someone figures out how to roll these services into one well marketed package, the costs can be rolled into monthly rental payments and a premium can be charged. Remember, these are the golden years for retirees and many do not want to sit around and be waited on – nor do they want to sit around and wait!

They want to be active and they and their adult children helping provide for them will gladly pay for great service whether it is an apartment or a single-family home!

Working with Seniors

As of 2015, the U.S. Census Bureau estimates that there are more than 47 million people above the age of 65 living in the United States. With a group of people this large, it is very difficult to make fair and accurate generalizations. In the United States, our senior citizen population is a melting pot of folks from all races, all incomes, all religions, and all walks of life. This means that there is an entire spectrum of seniors, from those who are rock-hardened criminals to modern-day Saints. When it comes to mobile homes, however, we investors often work with buyers looking for affordable housing—and possibly more modest accommodations.

Whether you are selling a mobile home to a senior buyer, renting it out, or even buying a mobile home from a senior citizen, there are important distinctions to remember. Senior sellers and buyers may be a bit different from sellers and buyers who are a bit younger and may be purchasing their first property. Please enlist the list below for help when dealing with senior mobile-home buyers, renters, and sellers.

Location

Senior citizens exist in all 50 states. When it comes to mobile-home parks, there are senior citizen communities throughout the entire country. These communities restrict the residents who are eligible to live inside the park to people over a specific age, whether it be 40 years old, 55 years old, 65 years old, etc. The age requirement is written into the rules and prospectus of the park.

Locally, be aware of the number of senior citizen only mobile home communities. Be aware of the mobile homes for sale in these communities and how many days they sat on the market prior to selling. Notice how the supply and demand changes at different times throughout the year. Because senior citizen mobile-home communities limit the age of buyers, it is crucial to have an accurate picture of supply and demand locally from senior buyers and sellers in your area.

Tip: The term "snowbird" typically refers to a senior citizen who leaves the colder states and heads for warmer states seasonally. This typically means that this type of senior has multiple homes, or rents a vacation home or mobile home while they are in the warmer states.

Related: How to Invest in Real Estate When Your Tenants Are Retired Seniors

Mobile Homes

Senior citizens are not weird or confusing. They are mostly rational people just like yourself. Some senior citizens are looking for extremely lavish mobile homes, while others are looking for much more humble and affordable accommodations for their golden years. Almost all senior citizens want to live in a safe and convenient area.

Repairs: As a general rule of thumb, most senior citizens would rather move into a clean and already livable mobile home than a fixer-upper.

Age: As a general rule of thumb, most senior citizens would rather move into a newer and modern mobile home than an older unit.

Number of bedrooms: As a general rule of thumb, most senior citizens are perfectly happy with a 2 bedroom mobile home compared with a larger home.

Sellers

Show respect. Senior citizen mobile-home sellers typically do not want to be rushed, belittled, or manipulated. Take extra time to listen to your seller's situation and provide help where needed. Aim to be a consultant when dealing with these sellers to educate them and let them know their options. Before making any purchase offers, make sure you are 100 percent certain on a realistic exit strategy and your comparable sales data.

Occasionally you may talk to people who are dealing with an age-related disease or illness. These diseases can cause forgetfulness, short tempers, and possible confusion. It is important to be open-minded, patient, and compassionate when dealing with these folks and their loved ones.

Buyers

No two senior buyers are the same. Some seniors will have money, and some will not. Some will be able to make repairs, and some will not. Many seniors will know exactly what they are talking, about and some will not. Of course, some may try to take advantage of you, while some will not. Always perform complete due diligence on every potential buyer you spend time with.

Some senior citizen buyers can be just as flaky and problematic as their 20-year-old counterparts. Make sure to always perform proper due diligence with all payment buyers regardless of their age, wealth, reputation, or social status.

Renters

Some of the best renters I know are senior citizens. It is true that many senior citizens are the recipients of Social Security, pension benefits, IRAs, and 401(k)s. This does not change the fact that some seniors will still mismanage their finances and delay monthly payments with a variety of excuses.

Furnished: In my experience there is no "general rule of thumb" when it comes to renting a furnished mobile home in a senior community. Some seniors will require, and be happy to pay extra for, a rental that is already fully furnished. Others will be providing their own furnishings.

In conclusion, with the baby boomers and every other subsequent generation getting older, there will not be a lack of senior customers now or in the future. While it is very difficult to make accurate generalizations concerning a group of more than 47 million Americans, we can certainly use common sense, experience, and prudent due-diligence practices to keep our clients and ourselves happy and safe.

CHAPTER 4
INVESTING IN MOBILE HOMES
WITH LESS THAN $25,000

It is hard to believe that the number one reason real estate investors start buying/selling used mobile homes is not the glamour and prestige. Many real estate investors begin purchasing; holding and/or reselling used mobile homes in parks due to the low perceived capital needed when getting started. While getting started investing with more cash is arguably better than starting poor, you may only need have a few thousand dollars to begin investing safely in used mobile homes inside pre-existing parks.

Do You Have Less Than $25,000 Available?

If you have less than $25,000 cash, it is safe to assume you will eventually exhaust 100 percent of your savings if you purchase and hold all mobile homes for rent/cash flow. It may take weeks or months to collect enough profit to purchase the next set of investment homes.

Let's avoid you running out of money while building up your cash flow business. If you are aiming to build a mobile home investing business with less than $25,000 to start, you will be doing the following.

Save as Much of Your Incoming Capital as Possible

Continue saving money from your other income sources to invest towards your real estate investing businesses. Remember that a successfully running real estate investing business should be converting some of your bank savings into long-term cash flow and/or bigger paydays.

Reinvest Profits

This is something almost all investors must do to continue operating an active and successful real estate business. Mobile home investing is no different. When starting with limited capital, you may wish to invest 100 percent of your profits back into your real estate business.

Practicality rating when starting with less than $25,000: Very practical. Do this for sure.

Seller Financing When Buying

Many sellers simply cannot accept payments when selling their manufactured homes. Some sellers may require a 30+% down payment from you before agreeing to owner financing. Some sellers may be much more eager and compromising, requiring only little down and low monthly payments. Aim to ask all mobile home sellers about purchasing their homes via some degree of seller-held financing. Using this method, we are oftentimes able to pay a considerable amount more for a home versus an all-cash purchase price.

Tip: Spend time understanding the sellers' wants and needs before making purchase offers. A seller will tell you their "wants" within the first 10 seconds of meeting them. In order to find out their "needs," you must spend time getting to know them and learning about what is going on in their lives and where they are moving to.

Practicality rating when starting with less than $25,000: Very practical when possible, depending on the sellers' needs.

Private Money

Friends, family members, other investors, and acquaintances are all examples of people who may be unhappy with their current rates of returns from banks, stocks, etc. These folks may consider lending you some money to gain a better return on their savings.

Practicality rating when starting with less than $25,000: Semi-practical. When getting started, few people may invest in you without a track record of proven successes in the field.

Capital Partners

A business partnership can take many forms. Perhaps you join forces with a silent partner only when you require extra capital, or perhaps this is a full-time partnership providing you capital for every deal. Remember that the investor taking all the action and creating the deal is likely the most valuable player.

Practicality rating when starting with less than $25,000: Practical, but be aware. Always have clarity with any potential partner. Understand everyone's roles, duties, and expectations on a day-to-day, week-to-week, and year-to-year basis.

Sell Mobile Homes for All Cash

Sell mobile homes for cash to raise money for future deals. Cash buyers want a great deal for their money. Depending on the time of the year and area of the country, selling a mobile home for all cash may be easier said than done. When selling a mobile home for all cash, you will be competing with almost every other mobile home seller looking for a local all-cash buyer.

Practicality rating when starting with less than $25,000: Semi-practical depending on the home, condition, location, and time of year.

Tip: When selling a used mobile home to an all-cash buyer, aim to at least double your invested capital.

Credit Cards, Helocs, or Banks

Credit cards provide cash advances, and Home Equity Lines of Credit provide liquid cash to millions of homeowners across the country. However, borrowing money to fund your real estate business may not necessarily be prudent.

Practicality rating when starting with less than $25,000: Not practical. Borrowing money to begin your investing career is a slippery slope. One reason for the risk is the small margin of error with regard to mobile homes inside parks. If you are just now beginning to invest, it is almost certain you will make many foolish/valuable mistakes while getting started and growing your portfolio. If you are using your own money, then these are simply valuable lessons learned. However, if you are using borrowed money, you will pay for these lessons for many more months to come every time you make a monthly loan payment.

Do You Have More Than $25,000 Available?

First things first, great job collecting and saving this amount of capital. Just because you have, this money does not mean you should spend it all in one location. From firsthand and secondhand experience, this $25,000 amount can purchase you at minimum four mobile homes, no matter which state you are located in (excluding Hawaii). However, after these first few properties, you may run out of capital to invest with unless you utilize some of the methods above.

CHAPTER 5
SINGLEWIDES OR DOUBLEWIDES

As an active mobile home investor, you will absolutely be talking to motivated mobile home sellers who own all sizes of mobile homes and manufactured homes. Some of these mobile homes will be considered singlewides, and others will be considered doublewides. Whether singlewide or doublewide, both of these sizes of mobile homes may be very profitable and in high demand by local buyers.

Sizes

Singlewide mobile homes are built no bigger than 18 feet wide and 90 feet long, with many singlewides you see running an average of 14' x 60'. Doublewide mobile homes on average are less than 40 feet wide and less than 90 feet long. Many doublewides you see may have an average dimension of 24' x 60'.

Supply

Through what research is available online and personally investing in mobile homes around the country, there absolutely seem to be more singlewide mobile homes in existence than doublewide homes — by a ratio of 3:1 in many areas. Likewise, there seem to be more 2-bedroom singlewides compared to 3-bedroom singlewides.

Disclaimer: The terms "mobile home" and "manufactured home" are being used interchangeably in this article. This is common not only throughout this article but throughout the real world with regard to mobile home investing. In reality, the term "manufactured home" is the verbiage used to describe most factory built housing constructed after 1976.

Demand

Demand changes as the purchasing opportunity changes. Larger cities may have more buying demand compared to smaller cities simply due to the increased number of people nearby looking for a new/used affordable home. Depending on whether you are selling this investment mobile home to an end user via an all cash sale or via monthly payments, the demand from buyers will change in most areas from singlewide to doublewide. Here's how.

Selling via All-Cash or Bank Financing: When selling a mobile home to an all-cash buyer or a bank financed buyer, you will be competing against many other mobile home sellers in the area also looking for an all-cash sale. If your mobile home is prettier and larger than the competition, your home will typically be purchased first, assuming the price is comparable. When selling for all-cash or bank financing, the bigger and more spacious home typically sells first (assuming the comparable location and park are relatively equal). In short, doublewides are more popular with a cash or bank-financed buyers. Bigger = Better.

Selling via Monthly Payments: With regard to selling used mobile homes via monthly payments, there is little difference with the purchasing demand from buyers when you are selling a singlewide mobile home versus a doublewide mobile home. The reason for this is simple — the attractiveness of the seller financing supersedes the need for a slightly more spacious home from buyers. In short, doublewides and singlewides are nearly equally popular when selling via monthly payments.

Repairs

Doublewide manufactured homes typically have double the square feet as compared to singlewide mobile homes. This means that there may be double the amount of rehabs needed with a doublewide mobile home versus a singlewide mobile home. More repairs needed inside the home on the floor, and more repairs needed outside of the home on the roof. The floor and roof of mobile homes are two costly areas to look for water stains, leaks, and damages.

Transporting

Singlewide mobile homes will typically cost less than half the amount to move and set up compared to a doublewide mobile home. Singlewide mobile homes will be moved as one complete unit in most cases, whereas doublewide mobile homes are typically transported in two separate halves once separated. These two halves must then be joined/reconnected at the home's new location.

Tip: Always, always, always hire a mobile home transporting company that comes with high recommendations and referrals. Aim to asked local mobile home park managers who they refer and trust to move in their mobile homes locally.

Mindset as a Mobile Home Investor

There is nothing inherently good or bad with a singlewide mobile home versus a doublewide mobile home. Both homes/deals may or may not be attractive to purchase. As active mobile home investors, we are looking to be both proactive and reactive to help local mobile home sellers and buyers. Aim to keep an open mind when speaking to local mobile home sellers and create a few offers to help sellers move on with their lives. Take into account all repairs, park approval processes, location, local market conditions, time of the year, age of the home, size, bedrooms, and more before making any purchase offers to any sellers.

Mindset as a Park Owner

From the perspective of a mobile home park owner, your community only has so much land and so many places to put mobile homes. A doublewide mobile home will cost double to purchase and move, plus consume double the amount of land as a singlewide. Still, they only typically generate the same amount in lot rent fees compared to a smaller singlewide. Even worse, a park owner may need to reduce the number of mobile home spaces if doublewides encroach onto their neighbors' pads. While doublewide mobile homes often may look more similar to single-family homes, there are always positives and negatives when adding larger homes to your community.

In conclusion, there is a buyer for most mobile homes you purchase. However, if you're not investing correctly, it can be easy to lose money and sacrifice profits. Remember that any mobile home you aim to resell should be attractive to a good section of society, as opposed to only a small handful of buyers, when reselling a mobile home. Before making purchase offers to sellers, know what local buyers will pay for any property you intend to invest in. Always know exactly what you are investing in before you purchase any home, and enter into every real estate transaction with clarity and understanding.

CHAPTER 6
OUT OF STATE INVESTING

The purpose of this is to educate you, a mobile home investor, to the realistic possibilities of investing outside of your comfortable driving territory. Below you will find some of the typical weekly and daily activities of an active mobile home investor. We will then discuss how these activities are affected when performed from states away.

Leads from Afar

Some leads you will absolutely be able to find without any boots on the ground. You have access to the same internet that everyone else has who is looking to purchase used mobile homes in your desired area. Online sites such as Craigslist and Zillow are popular databases to locate current sellers.

The reality: Without employees on the ground or a partner with a vested interest in your deals, you will likely be missing out on many profitable mobile home seller leads. Personal mobile home investing experience has taught me that a majority of closed leads do not come from the internet and are not publicly advertised. Many leads are found before the general public knows the home is for sale. This may be done by being well known in the area, using consistent marketing, networking, and regularly meeting with new sellers to make offers.

Talking with Sellers Via Phone

Talking with sellers and understanding their situation can absolutely be performed successfully over the telephone. An investor may also be able to build reporter, negotiate, and receive email pictures of the property without ever meeting the seller face-to-face. Some motivated sellers will absolutely be willing to close with a potential buyer (you) without ever meeting you. These sellers will be more concerned with getting paid and less concerned with your wants. In short, introducing yourself, building rapport, making offers, negotiating, looking over pictures and more can all be done successfully over the phone.

The reality: For consistent investing long-term, it will be wise to have your business partner or yourself physically present to meet sellers face-to-face and shake hands.

Due Diligence When Purchasing

To this day, I like to see things for myself and kick the tires before buying. The next best thing to my own eyes inspecting a property is having someone I trust or have trained inspect a mobile home properly. This person could be a property inspector, trusted handyman, several different handymen, and/or a partner with a vested interest in the property.

Tip: If you hire someone hourly to perform your due diligence, make sure to verify everything they are looking over for their first few deals. Hourly employees are not nearly as invested in a property as a partner who is splitting profits and expenses with you.

Funding Out-of-State

In theory, money can be sent around the globe instantly. Whether you are funding the deal yourself, utilizing the help of a local* credit union, or borrowing the money from Uncle Frank's IRA, this can be done from almost anywhere around the country.

*If working with a local credit union, it certainly may be helpful to be local to the business's location.

Closing Out-Of-State

One final walk-through prior to closing is advised with any investment property you are purchasing. This may be outsourced to someone you trust or a professional inspection company for a fee. Additionally, unless you are using a closing attorney, escrow office or title agent, it will be you or your partner's responsibility to make sure all paperwork is successfully signed and all keys are taken before money is handed to the seller(s).

Tip: If purchasing within a pre-existing mobile home park, remember that many park managers will allow you to start the background approval process via the phone/fax/internet. However, many communities will insist that you or your partner be able to meet and sign a copy of the park's rules and lease agreement before purchasing a home in the community.

Repairs and Outsourcing

Many investors I speak with have already come to the realization that they will be hiring someone more experienced than themselves to perform manual labor and make the needed repairs on the property. While paying someone to perform repairs is the easy part, finding and managing a quality handyman or contractor who shows up and performs as agreed may prove difficult. Having someone local on the ground to report back to you with pictures daily may be crucial. This person may be the local community manager, a neighbor, a business partner, or the handymen themselves.

Understand your exit strategy and really know what your buyers want in a used mobile home. Do not make unnecessary improvements that will not bring back their value plus a noticeable profit.

Reselling/Renting From Abroad

Your selling game plan and selling funnel can be created and thought through from the comfort of your own home. You may choose to have sellers call you directly, or you can send them to your selling agent or prerecorded phone message describing the property and qualification details. You may then be able to have the potential tenants or buyers walk through the property with the help of a lockbox on the front door. They may even fill out a credit application online, paid for with their own credit card. In short, the modern age makes it possible to not need to meet your potential tenant or tenant-buyer before the closing date unless desired by you or the tenant.

Tip: Utilizing the help of a property manager and/or online tenant screening service can be extremely valuable to streamlining your renting/selling process. The help of a qualified mortgage loan originator will be equally as important for screening buyers and preparing paperwork when reselling a mobile home with owner financing.

Management

Occasional issues may arise; however, if the mobile home is located in a pre-existing mobile home park, the current park manager may solve many of these issues. Having someone local to post notices, knock on doors, inspect possible repairs needed, and drive-by properties can be super valuable to your day-to-day business. Possible sources of help for outsourcing may be local property management companies, experienced real estate agent friends, semi-experienced family members, or a vested real estate investing partner.

There are so many ways to make money in real estate investing, and many of them produce results with correct daily action. When investing in mobile homes outside of your comfortable driving territory, you give up the ability to be on location as much as you may like. Before proceeding forward, make sure you truly understand not only what will be required when things are going good, but more importantly, what actions and responsibilities will be required when things do not go as planned.

CHAPTER 7
INVESTORS ANXIETY, WASTED TIME & LOST PROFIT

The 3 scenarios below are quite common, and it is likely you will see these same situations in parks near you while trying to purchase mobile homes. While many mobile home parks and park managers are rational, friendly, and welcoming to their residents, other community managers care little for their residents and only for the bottom line.

While reading the situations below, try to mentally place yourself in these 3 scenarios. The bullet points raised below can cause you anxiety, lost time, and lost profit if not watched out for. Do not let this happen to you. After reading the list below, please keep these in your mind in the event you find yourself looking at purchasing mobile homes inside one of these types of parks.

Strict Application Park

While dealing with mobile homes inside a mobile home community, it is important to note that each park owner may dictate who lives within their walls. Most parks are reasonable in their application criteria — such as a credit scores over

550, income two to four times the lot rent payment, no evictions, and reasonable/minimal credit or criminal blemishes. However, some parks are irrational and far too strict in their requirements for residents.

Lesson: In the beginning of my career, I invested within a mobile home community that required a minimum credit beacon score of 700 to be approved to live in the park. The community also required a 4-page application requesting detailed employment verification for the past four years, past housing, references, bank information, automobile information, etc. I had too little experience to know that these "much stricter than usual" requirements from this park would make it very difficult to resell the home.

The mobile home spoke for itself. The property was beautiful, and it was purchased by my company for a very low price. I know now that the price was so low due to the difficulty in finding an approved buyer. When the home was advertised, it had no shortage of potential buyers wanting the property. The trouble came after the potential buyers left the home and headed to the park office for approval. Once finding out about the high criteria and high application fee the park demanded, few ever followed through with an application. After two month of holding the home, I began offering to pay for verbally qualified buyers to run their applications. I paid for six application fees before a family of two was approved for the park. I took a discount on the home when I resold, collected my profits, and have never done business in this park again.

Important to note was that I met a number of other sellers who were having the same complaint about selling their homes in this park. These homes could have been purchased for a big discount; however, the hassle and time to try to resell would have not been worth the immediate upfront savings. Removing the homes from this park to another piece of land or friendlier park may make sense in this scenario.

Semi-Empty Park

Imagine you are driving through an established mobile home community you have never been to before. You notice that there are approximately 25% or more of the existing pads free of mobile homes. This could be for a number of reasons.

- Transitional Period: The Park may have recently kicked out a majority of the less desirable owners and/or homes in the park, thereby cleaning up the quality of the park. This happens when new management or ownership takes control of a loosely operated park. If this is the case, there is little to be concerned about.

- Poor Ownership and/or Management: Another reason many mobile home owners may choose to remove their homes from a community may be that unhappy living conditions exist due to hostile park management or unreasonably high lot rent fees.

Lesson: I have only seen this twice. The community residents rationally and almost unanimously despised the park management enough to cause many owners to pay to have their mobile homes moved out of a park they have lived in for years. If a park manager is too strict, bossy, demanding, prejudiced, negligent, and/or greedy for too long, this could cause a mass exodus in a community. If you get this impression from local residents or park managers, strongly reconsider a long-term relationship with this park.

Rude Management Park

Most park managers are caring and rational people just like you. In addition, they oftentimes have thankless jobs and give much of themselves to their local communities. Much of the time when you correctly approach park managers aiming to help, they are approachable and willing to discuss business with you. However, sometimes park managers are in a bad mood or may be busy. When meeting a park manager for the first time, be aware that you are screening this person as well as the park itself. You will be forming a relationship with this park manager, and it is important you both like and respect each other.

Lesson: Without meeting the manager a few times, it is difficult to say whether or not this park manager is always happy, rude, greedy, bossy, etc. Instead, plan to interact with the park manager at least three times before you purchase a mobile home within any community.

In short, there are many moving parts to every decision that goes into whether or not you should invest in any property. When a mobile home is located in a mobile home community, this only adds to the variable of factors to consider. If you have further questions, do not hesitate to reach out below.

CHAPTER 8
MOBILE HOME BUILDERS AND DEALERS

Mobile homes offer investors a great deal of flexibility and affordability when it comes to building up profit and value. Below we will be focusing on walking through your local mobile home builders, dealer showrooms, and repo lots to learn more and make you money.

Let us first understand the difference between a mobile home builder, dealer showroom, and mobile home repo lot.

- Dealer showroom: This may be a nationwide company or local mom-and-pop dealer that owns a "lot" with show homes to walk through. These homes may be new from the factory or pre-owned homes. If the mobile homes are used, they are likely there due to trade-in or purchase on a secondary market.
- Mobile home builder: This generally refers to the factory and distribution center for a particular builder of mobile homes. These buildings and showrooms are typically

large and only offer one maker of mobile homes. Examples: Clayton, Fleetwood, Redman, Champion, Jacobson, etc.

- Mobile home repo lot: This is likely a local dealer that specializes in selling used mobile homes. Typically, you may find homes with various level of rehab needed. Look for the word "repo" on the entrance sign or business card to identify these dealers.

You can network with dealers and ask questions.

While you're walking through each home, you can ask specific questions from the dealer about each home to better know your product, design, flaws, etc. Whether learning about a builder, local moving laws, price specials, specific home questions, knowledge is power.

Know Your Product

Know what you sell or will be selling — affordable housing. Although we are not investing in these specific mobile homes, we can learn much from them. Especially if you are newer to manufactured housing, I highly recommend walking through, touching, smelling, and looking inside and out of these new and used mobile homes.

You'll get excited about the new amenities modern manufactured homes have.

As an investor, the average mobile home I invest in is roughly 8-20 years old. While these homes oftentimes have walk-in closets, skylights, kitchen islands, garden tubs, and even his and her bathroom sinks, these decade-old homes pale in comparison to brand new manufactured homes and new features and amenities.

Know Local Movers

Dealers know movers. These are recommended movers you can get referrals for when you may need to move a mobile home in the future.

You Can Sell to Them

Dealers are in a business to buy low and sell high. If you can sell them a mobile home for an attractive price, many dealers will act quickly.

While in the office, find out from this dealer what homes they will purchase. Age? Size? Location? Price? Aim to speak with the manager in charge.

You can explore how they can work with you.

Dealers often work with vacant landowners. Whether you have a vacant, unimproved parcel of land or a piece of land that is all-ready for a mobile home, you have a valuable piece of property for the right buyer. Dealers often keep lists of land for sale in case a qualified mobile home buyer needs a vacant lot.

CHAPTER 9
MOBILE HOME FINANCING

Securing traditional financing for mobile homes and manufactured homes can sometimes seem difficult, especially in our current economical market. Whether the mobile home is new to you or being refinanced, lenders typically have stricter underwriting guidelines than more traditional site build homes.

Building codes changed in late 2005 after the severe hurricane season experienced in the Southern states. Mobile homes built after this date must follow a strict set of building guidelines; this helps to insure safety and a longer life span for those mobile homes built just months before. Safety improvements include stronger construction materials that better resist moisture, wind and fire, extra cross beams for support, plus dozens of additional building improvements.

Given this info, lets examine the various options available for financing your mobile home purchases.

MOBILE HOME FINANCING OPTIONS

- Government Backed Loans
- Conventional Financing
- Private Lenders
- Seller Financing

Government Backed Loans

If you are interested in a brand new mobile home, then a local mobile home dealer or mobile home community will be able to direct you to a nearby financing agency/broker. They will approve you for a certain amount based on your credit history, job record, amount down, current debt, savings, etc. You can then take this approved amount to any mobile home dealer and purchase the new mobile home you want.

The Federal Housing Administration (FHA) and Veterans Association (VA) both have some level of financing available for mobile homes/manufactured homes. The subject property must be located or moved on a suitable site and attached to the ground conforming to current safety codes. Mobile homes attached to rented lots in a rented park may be approved if the mobile home community complies with FHA guidelines.

Conventional Financing

Most conventional lenders will not loan money to mobile homes located within a rented mobile home community. There is simply too much risk (I will explain why a little later). However, you can find conventional lenders that will lend to mobile homes with land (meaning the land is owned by the borrower). Some requirements I have found in the past are that the subject mobile home is less than 15 years old, the borrower has 10%-20% down, over a 620 FICO score and an excellent job history.

A subset of conventional loans is the sub-prime lending market, meaning the borrower has less than perfect credit history, typically a FICO score below 620. The sub-prime market has its own lenders that specialize in financing mobile homes on land and within rented parks — requirements vary by lender. These subprime lenders offer mobile home loans with high interest rates, higher down payments, additional fees and typically shorter terms than conventional or government loans. (10 years VS. 30 years)

Private Lenders

Anyone that has extra money, a bloated IRA or specializes in privately lending money may offer a loan on just about any home, if the terms are in the private lenders favor. A great way to find private lenders is to attend a local real estate club meeting and ask others. Private lenders have to conform to certain government lending requirements to avoid fraud, but can decide which homes they choose to invest in based on any requirements they choose at any particular time. If you currently own a piece of land (free & clear) that is ready for a mobile home, many private lenders will lend money if the attached land is placed as collateral. However owning the land outright is not usually a requirement.

I personally made a private loan to a friend of mine; in exchange, I recorded a note and mortgage against the property so I was protected. I held possession of the Title to the mobile home until the time he planned to pay me off. The old adage is correct, never do business with friends. My friend of many years ended up not being able to pay. I took possession of the home without foreclosing but I lost a good friend in exchange.

Seller Financing

Seller financing really is not a type of lending, however it is an extremely important tool for any serious real estate investor. Why is seller held financing not a type of lending? Seller financing IS NOT the seller lending you money, no money ever changes hands. Instead, it is simply the terms of the sale. The seller is accepting payments for the purchase price of his/her home.

I am happy to say that I have never personally utilized traditional financing to purchase any mobile home. I always structure financing with the owner of the mobile home I am interested in purchasing. Seller financing is easy to structure; there are no credit check and typically, I make no down payment. When working with a motivated seller you structure the terms of the financing, not the other way around like traditional financing.

Note: The reason for the statement earlier, "It is risky for Government, conventional, sub-prime and private lenders to lend money to mobile home inside rented parks" is for the fact that the land is not owned by the borrower. Let role-play. Let us say you are a lender, and you lend money to a borrower who purchases a mobile home inside a rented park. The borrower loses his or her job and cannot make the monthly payments to both you and the park. It is bad enough that now you are not being paid on your Note, but now you have to pay the park's lot/pad rent or risk having your home evicted. If the borrower continues to not pay you must foreclose, continue to pay the lot rent every month and attract a new buyer that is already park approved. Banks and lending companies make money by lending their money and collecting an interest rate. They are not in the real estate business. Most conventional lenders never want to worry about the burden of filling an empty home inside a park.

SAMPLE CONTRACT FOR DEED

SALES CONTRACT / CONTRACT FOR DEED

THIS DAY this agreement is entered into by and between

_____

_____, hereinafter referred to as "SELLER", whether one or more, and [BUYER NAME], hereinafter referred to as "PURCHASER", whether one or more, on the terms and conditions and for the purposes hereinafter set forth:

1.

SALE OF PROPERTY

For and in consideration of TEN DOLLARS ($10.00) and other good and valuable considerations the receipt and sufficiency of which is hereby acknowledged, Seller does hereby agree to convey, sell, assign, transfer and set over unto Purchaser, the following property situated in _____ County, State of Texas, said property being described as follows: *(Type description or attach description as exhibit "A")*

_____

_____

_____

Together with all rights of ownership associated with the property, including, but not limited to, all easements and rights benefiting the premises, whether or not such easements and rights are of record, and all tenements, hereditaments, improvements and appurtenances, including all lighting fixtures, plumbing fixtures, shades, venetian blinds, curtain rods, storm windows, storm doors, screens, awnings, if any, and now on the premises._____

_____

SUBJECT TO all recorded easements, rights-of-way, conditions, encumbrances and limitations and to all applicable building and use restrictions, zoning laws and ordinances, if any, affecting the property.

2.

PURCHASE PRICE AND TERMS

The purchase price of the property shall be $
_____. The purchaser does hereby agree to
pay to the order of the Seller the sum of
_____ Dollars ($
_____) upon execution of this agreement, with the
balance of $_____being due and payable as
follows:(Select one)

[   ] (a) **Cash Sale:** The full purchase price upon the
delivery of a recordable Warranty Deed conveying title in
the condition provided for herein.

[   ] (b) **New Mortgage:** The full purchase price
upon the delivery of a recordable Warranty Deed
conveying title in the condition provided for herein,
contingent upon Purchaser's ability to obtain a
mortgage amortized for no less than   years, in the
amount of   % of purchase price on or before the
date the sale is to be closed, which Purchaser agrees to
apply for financing by

 (Date)

Purchaser agrees to use his or her best efforts to obtain
such financing. Purchaser agrees to pay any and all costs
that are a condition of financing, unless otherwise agreed
therein. **IF SAID MORTGAGE FINANCING IS NOT
APPROVED BY** (Date)   At   **AM/PM,
SELLER HAS OPTION TO DECLARE PURCHASER'S
DEFAULT AND TO TERMINATE THIS**

AGREEMENT BY WRITTEN NOTICE TO PURCHASER. A certificate of pre-approval presented by the Purchaser, does not necessarily guaranty financing.

[   ] (c) **Sale to Existing Financing or Land Contract:** Upon execution and delivery of [   ] a recordable Special Warranty Deed and subject to existing financing.

[   ] Assignment of vendee interest in land contract. Purchaser to pay the difference (approximately $) between the purchase price and the balance as of day of closing, of said mortgage or land contract bearing interest at   % per annum and with monthly payments of $ which do   do not   include tax and/or insurance, which Purchaser assumes and agrees to pay. Purchaser agrees to reimburse Seller for any funds held in escrow. Purchaser to pay all taxes and insurance costs if not included in the monthly payment stated above. **SELLER UNDERSTANDS THAT THE SALE OR TRANSFER OF THE PROPERTY DESCRIBED IN THIS AGREEMENT MAY NOT RELIEVE THE SELLER OF ANY LIABILITY THAT SELLER MAY HAVE UNDER THE MORTGAGE(S) OR LAND CONTRACT(S) TO WHICH THE PROPERTY IS SUBJECT, UNLESS OTHERWISE AGREED TO BY THE LENDER OR VENDOR OR REQUIRED BY LAW OR REGULATION.**

[   ] (d) **Land Contract:** The down payment of   ($) Dollars and the execution of land contract, acknowledging payment of that sum and calling for the payment of the remainder of the purchase money of $ in   payments of $ or more, which (SHALL) (SHALL NOT) include interest payment at the rate of   percent per annum, and which (SHALL)   (SHALL NOT)   include prepaid taxes and insurance. The contract shall be paid in full on or before   years from date of sale. Purchaser agrees to provide Seller a recent credit report acceptable to the sellers.

If interest is charged, interest shall be computed monthly and deducted from payment and the balance of payment shall be applied on principal.

3.

TIME OF THE ESSENCE

Time is of the essence in the performance of each and every term and provision in this agreement by Purchaser.

4.

SECURITY

This contract shall stand as security of the payment of the obligations of Purchaser.

5.

MAINTENANCE OF IMPROVEMENTS

All improvements on the property, including, but not limited to, buildings, trees or other improvements now on the premises, or hereafter made or placed thereon, shall be a part of the security for the performance of this contract and shall not be removed therefrom. Purchaser shall not commit, or suffer any other person to commit, any waste or damage to said premises or the appurtenances and shall keep the premises and all improvements in as good condition as they are now.

6.

CONDITION OF IMPROVEMENTS

Purchaser agrees that the Seller has not made, nor makes any representations or warranties as to the condition of the premises, the condition of the buildings, appurtenances and fixtures locate thereon, and/or the location of the boundaries. Purchaser accepts the property in it's "as-is" condition without warranty of any kind.

7.

POSSESSION OF PROPERTY

Purchaser shall take possession of the property and all improvements thereon upon execution of this contract and shall continue in the peaceful enjoyment of the property so long as all payments due under the terms of this contract are timely made. Purchaser agrees to keep the property in a good state of repair and in the event of termination of this contract, Purchaser agrees to return the property to Seller in substantially the same condition as it now exists, ordinary wear and tear excepted. Seller reserves the right to inspect the property at any time with or without notice to Purchaser.

8.

TAXES, INSURANCE AND ASSESSMENTS

Taxes and Assessments: During the term of this contract :(Select one)

(__) (a) Purchaser shall pay all taxes and assessments levied against the property.

(__) (b) Seller shall pay all taxes and assessments levied against the property. In the event that Seller pays the taxes and insurance, Purchaser shall reimburse Purchaser for same upon 30 day notice to purchaser

Content Insurance: Purchaser shall be solely responsible for obtaining insurance of the contents insuring contents owned by Purchaser. Seller shall be solely responsible for obtaining insurance on all contents owned by Seller.

Liability and Hazard Insurance: Liability insurance shall be maintained by Purchaser during the term of this contract naming Seller as an additional insured, in the amount of not less than $_____.

Fire, Hazard and Windstorm insurance: Fire, hazard and windstorm insurance shall be maintained as follows: (Select)

(__) (a) Purchaser shall obtain fire, hazard and windstorm insurance in the amount not less than $_____, on a policy of insurance naming Seller as additional insured.

(__) (b) Seller shall obtain and pay for hazard, fire and windstorm insurance in an amount not less than $_____. In the event Seller elects this option, Purchaser shall repay the amount so paid by Seller within thirty (30) days of demand for same by Seller.

Should the Purchaser fail to pay any tax or assessment, or installment thereof, when due, or keep said buildings insured, Seller may pay the same and have the buildings insured, and the amounts thus expended shall be a lien on said premises and may be added to the balance then unpaid, or collected by Seller, in the discretion if Seller with interest until paid at the rate of the ___ per cent per annum.

In case of any damage as a result of which said insurance proceeds are available, the Purchaser may, within sixty (60) days of said loss or damage, give to the Seller written notice of Purchaser's election to repair or rebuild the damaged parts of the premises, in which event said insurance proceeds shall be used for such purpose. The balance of said proceeds, if any, which remain after completion of said repairing or rebuilding, or all of said insurance proceeds if the Purchaser elects not to repair or rebuild, shall be applied first toward the satisfaction of any existing defaults under the terms of this contract, and then as a prepayment upon the principal balance owing. No such prepayment shall defer the time for payment of any remaining payments required by said contract. Any surplus of said proceeds in excess of the balance owing hereon shall be paid to the Purchaser.

9.

DEFAULT

If the Purchaser shall fail to perform any of the covenants or conditions contained in this contract on or before the date on which the performance is required, the Seller shall give Purchaser notice of default or performance, stating the Purchaser is allowed fourteen (14) days from the date of the Notice to cure the default or performance. In the event the default or failure of performance is not cured within the 14 day time period, then Seller shall have any of the following remedies, in the discretion of Seller:

(a) give the Purchaser a written notice specifying the failure to cure the default and informing the Purchaser that if the default continues for a period of an additional fifteen (15) days after service of the notice of failure to cure, that without further notice, this contract shall stand cancelled and Seller may regain possession of the property as provided herein; or

(b) give the Purchaser a written notice specifying the failure to cure the default and informing the Purchaser that if the default continues for a period of an additional fifteen (15) days after service of the notice of failure to cure, that without further notice, the entire principal balance and unpaid interest shall be immediately due and payable and Seller may take appropriate action against Purchaser for collection of same according to the laws of the State of Texas.

In the event of default in any of the terms and conditions or installments due and payable under the terms of this contract and Seller elects 9(a), Seller shall be entitled to immediate possession of the property.

In the event of default and termination of the contract by Seller, Purchaser shall forfeit any and all payments made under the terms of this contract including taxes and assessments as liquidated damages, Seller shall be entitled to recover such other damages as they may be due which are caused by the acts or negligence of Purchaser.

The parties expressly agree that in the event of default not cured by the Purchaser and termination of this agreement, and Purchaser fails to vacate the premises, Seller shall have the right to obtain possession by appropriate court action.

10.

DEED AND EVIDENCE OF TITLE

Upon total payment of the purchase price and any and all late charges, and other amounts due Seller, Seller agrees to deliver to Purchaser a Special Warranty Deed to the subject property, as Sellers expense, free and clear of any liens or encumbrances other than taxes and assessments for the current year.

11.

<u>NOTICES</u>

All notices required hereunder shall be deemed to have been made when deposited in the U. S. Mail, postage prepaid, certified, return receipt requested, to the Purchaser or Seller at the addresses listed below. All notices required hereunder may he sent to:

Seller:

_____

_____

_____

Purchaser:

_____

_____

_____

and when mailed, postage prepaid, to said address, shall be binding and conclusively presumed to be served upon said parties respectively.

12.

ASSIGNMENT OR SALE

Purchaser [   ] may or [   ] may not sell, assign, transfer or convey any interest in the subject property or this agreement, without securing consent of the Seller.

13.

PREPAYMENT

Purchaser to have the right to prepay, without penalty, the whole or any part of the balance remaining unpaid on this contract at any time before the due date.

14.

ATTORNEY FEES

In the event of default, Purchaser shall pay to Seller, Seller's reasonable and actual attorneys' fees and expenses incurred by Seller in enforcement of any rights of Seller. All attorney fees shall be payable prior to Purchaser's being deemed to have corrected any such default.

15.

LATE PAYMENT CHARGES

If Purchaser shall fail to pay, within fifteen (15) days after due date, any installment due hereunder, Purchaser shall be required to pay an additional charge of five (5%) percent of the late installment. Such charge shall be paid to Seller at the time of payment of the past due installment.

16.

CONVEYANCE OR MORTGAGE BY SELLER

If the Seller's interest is now or hereafter encumbered by mortgage, the Seller covenants that Seller will meet the payments of principal and interest thereon as they mature and produce evidence thereof to the Purchaser upon demand. In the event the Seller shall default upon any such mortgage or land contract, the Purchaser shall have the right to do the acts or make the payments necessary to cure such default and shall be reimbursed for so doing by receiving, automatically, credit to this contract to apply on the payments due or to become due hereon.

The Seller reserves the right to convey, his or her interest in the above described land and such conveyance hereof shall not be a cause for rescission but such conveyance shall be subject to the terms of this agreement.

The Seller may, during the lifetime of this contract, place a mortgage on the premises above described, which shall be a lien on the premises, superior to the rights of the Purchaser herein, or may continue and renew any existing mortgage thereon, provided that the aggregate amount due on all outstanding mortgages shall not at any time be greater than the unpaid balance of the contract.

17.

ENTIRE AGREEMENT

This Agreement embodies and constitutes the entire understanding between the parties with respect to the transactions contemplated herein. All prior or contemporaneous agreements, understandings, representations, oral or written, are merged into this Agreement.

18.

AMENDMENT – WAIVERS

This Agreement shall not be modified, or amended except by an instrument in writing signed by all parties.

No delay or failure on the part of any party hereto in exercising any right, power or privilege under this Agreement or under any other documents furnished in connection with or pursuant to this Agreement shall impair any such right, power or privilege or be construed as a waiver of any default or any acquiescence therein. No single or partial exercise of any such right, power or privilege shall preclude the further exercise of such right, power or privilege, or the exercise of any other right, power or privilege. No waiver shall be valid against any party hereto unless made in writing and signed by the party against whom enforcement of such waiver is sought and then only to the extent expressly specified therein.

19.

SEVERABILITY

If any one or more of the provisions contained in this Agreement shall be held illegal or unenforceable by a court, no other provisions shall be affected by this holding. The parties intend that in the event one or more provisions of this agreement are declared invalid or unenforceable, the remaining provisions shall remain enforceable and this agreement shall be interpreted by a Court in favor of survival of all remaining provisions.

20.

HEADINGS

Section headings contained in this Agreement are inserted for convenience of reference only, shall not be deemed to be a part of this Agreement for any purpose, and shall not in any way define or affect the meaning, construction or scope of any of the provisions hereof.

21.

PRONOUNS

All pronouns and any variations thereof shall be deemed
to refer to the masculine, feminine, neuter, singular, or
plural, as the identity of the person or entity may require.
As used in this agreement: (1) words of the masculine
gender shall mean and include corresponding neuter
words or words of the feminine gender, (2) words in the
singular shall mean and include the plural and vice versa,
and (3) the word "may" gives sole discretion without any
obligation to take any action.

22.

JOINT AND SEVERAL LIABILITY

All Purchasers, if more than one, covenants and agrees
that their obligations and liability shall be joint and
several.

23.

PURCHASER'S RIGHT TO REINSTATE AFTER ACCELERATION

If Purchaser defaults and the loan is accelerated, then
Purchaser shall have the right of reinstatement as allowed
under the laws of the State of Texas, provided that
Purchaser: (a) pays Lender all sums which then would be
due under this agreement as if no acceleration had

occurred; (b) cures any default of any other covenants or agreements; and (c) pays all expenses incurred in enforcing this agreement, including, but not limited to, reasonable attorneys' fees, and other fees incurred for the purpose of protecting Seller's interest in the Property and rights under this agreement. Seller may require that Purchaser pay such reinstatement sums and expenses in one or more of the following forms, as selected by Seller: (a) cash, (b) money order, (c) certified check, bank check, treasurer's check or cashier's check, provided any such check is drawn upon an institution whose deposits are insured by a federal agency, instrumentality or entity or (d) Electronic Funds Transfer. Upon reinstatement by Purchaser, this Security Instrument and obligations secured hereby shall remain fully effective as if no acceleration had occurred.

24.

<u>HEIRS AND ASSIGNS</u>

This contract shall be binding upon and to the benefit of the heirs, administrators, executors, and assigns of the parties hereto. However, nothing herein shall authorize a transfer in violation of paragraph (12).

25.

<u>OTHER PROVISIONS</u>

_____

_____

_____

_____

_____

WITNESS THE SIGNATURES of the Parties this the

___ day of _____, 20___.

SELLER:

_____

_____

PURCHASER:

_____

_____

STATE OF _____

COUNTY OF _____

The instrument was acknowledged before me on

_____ (date), by

_____(nam

e(s)).

_____

                                        Notary Public

                Printed Name: _____

My Commission Expires:

_____

STATE OF _____

COUNTY OF _____

The instrument was acknowledged before me on

_____(date), by

_____(na

me(s)).

_____

Notary Public

Printed Name: _____

My Commission Expires:

_____

CHAPTER 10
MOBILE HOME SELLERS VS TRADITIONAL HOME SELLERS

It may not come to any surprise to hear that mobile home sellers and manufactured home sellers are quite different from traditional "site built" home sellers. Your rationale may be that if mobile homes were significantly different from traditional single family homes, then why wouldn't the sellers be unique and different as well? In the quick list below, let us explore both common and unorthodox ways these mobile home sellers can be unique.

Many manufactured home sellers have a finite date set in their minds as to when they need to leave their properties. Many sellers know that they will not or cannot continue to pay for monthly mobile home park lot rent past a certain month if they can help it. While some mobile home sellers are financially, sound and not in a rush to sell, many mobile home sellers are paycheck to paycheck-type sellers who cannot afford to pay multiple bills on a property they are not even living in any longer. There are, of course, always exceptions to the rule, and the above are very general statements.

- They still require due diligence.

All sellers, real estate or otherwise, have the ability to stretch the truth, tell white lies, and omit facts about a property they are looking to sell. This bullet point is not technically a valid one; however, this bullet point is to express the fact that human nature is in all of us, no matter where we live or what we are selling. Please do not incorrectly think that because someone is from a lower socioeconomic background that he or she is more or less prone to deceit. There are good and bad apples in every bunch. Always perform thorough due diligence on every mobile home or single family home you are looking to invest in.

- They may be looking at fewer options.

Many mobile home parks and mobile home communities have restrictions on how mobile homes may be purchased and resold within their walls. In many mobile home communities, this eliminates the possibility of a lease option, contract for title, or other creative payment arrangement that does not convey title to a new buyer on day one.

With this said, mobile homes in parks typically have fewer options to be purchased and resold than traditional site built property on land you own. When you own the land, you do not need to worry about a park's approval process and/or approval criteria. Even though there are fewer options when purchasing and reselling, many buyers and sellers still have the possibility to owner finance, bank finance, or even rent a subject property inside of a pre-existing community.

- There is a higher need for investors' help.

In almost every area around the country, there are more mobile home sellers located in pre-existing parks than there are cash buyers. Cash buyers are few and far between in many areas around the country, especially when compared to buyers that are willing to pay via seller held financing. There are even fewer mobile home investors who are actively looking to help local sellers and work with parks in your area. It is for this reason that many mobile home investors are greeted with open arms and eager ears from local sellers in most markets. When mobile home investors correctly positions themselves, they are often one of the few offers that some sellers will ever receive to purchase their used mobile homes.

- Mobile home sellers may be more interested in building rapport.

People are people. Some sellers have the gift of gab, while others are very direct and to the point. You will have 10-minute appointments with traditional site-built single family homes and also with regard to mobile home sellers. Conversely, you will also go to many 2+ hour first appointments with single family home sellers as well as mobile home sellers. One strong correlation is the more motivated and emotional the seller, the longer the first appointment with a seller may go. This is often due to the fact that we investors will be listening to problems the seller is currently struggling with in regard to selling their property, as well as what these sellers are looking for moving forward.

While there are a variety of motivated sellers in any given market, mobile home sellers may have a greater need to keep communicating with you and building rapport so you are encouraged to make them a purchase offer(s) on their properties. Simply said, a high percentage of mobile home sellers will be happy and eager to build rapport with you simply because you are one of the few people willing to listen and help in their situation.

- They may be thriftier.

This bullet point is certainly debatable; however, I have heard many of my mobile home buyers comment and smile gladly when they realize they are purchasing a good quality used manufactured home for less than $30 per square foot, compared to the single family home they just downsized from, where they were $100+ per square foot. While every purchaser of a mobile home is different, this certainly can add to a owners'/sellers' mindset when it comes to selling and/or buying their properties. Depending on the sellers' mindset, this may affect the sales price and flexibility of the sellers positively or negatively from an investor's point of view.

In conclusion, every bullet point above can be disproven and shown incorrect in certain cases. Every mobile home seller is different, and no two deals are exactly alike. People's needs and motivations change regularly, while homes, rules, and demand vary from location to location. One thing is for sure, assuming you live within the continental United States, there are mobile home sellers in and around your area who are confused as to why their homes have not sold yet and why more people are not coming to look at their properties for sale. These sellers may become frustrated at their confusions and may be eager to hear from a local mobile home investing expert who knows about the local market and can help concerning their properties.

CHAPTER 11
COMMON PROBLEMS WITH OLDER MOBILE HOMES

As an active mobile home investor, you will likely walk through older and newer mobile homes. Over the decades, more and more regulations have been instituted regarding the manufacturing of factory built homes, resulting in better and better quality. However, after a home has been lived in for years and possibly decades, some problems and repair issues may arise that you will want to notice as an investor.

Sinking Foundation

A mobile home's foundation will vary from area to area and home to home. Local mobile home movers may follow current local codes—or they may not. Some areas allow for your investment mobile home to sit atop a peer and beam foundation, while others allow for your property to be supported by concrete blocks sitting on top of crushed rock. Still others allow for additional foundation options.

Ultimately, if the foundation is not sturdy enough, situated correctly, or on a concrete slab (permanent foundation), a mobile home's support may sink slowly into the earth over time. Add soft ground or wet weather, and this sinking action can speed up. In most cases, this is not a deal-breaker when purchasing a used mobile home.

Tip: Raising a mobile home is a common task that may need to be performed every now and then to specific mobile homes you purchase. An experienced mobile home handyman or mobile home mover will be able to raise/level a mobile home in the matter of a few hours or days with the right tools.

Doors Not Aligning

A common side effect to a mobile home sinking is that the main front and back doors may not line up or close correctly any longer. Keep in mind that when a home sinks, it will typically be just on one side of the home or one set of peers that are sinking into the ground. This will cause the home to be lopsided and put unnecessary stress on one side of the mobile home.

Windows/Walls Leaking

Water is a natural enemy of mobile homes. Always check under every exterior window, as well as on the entire interior perimeter of a mobile home. Overflowing gutters, a leaking roof, or holes in the siding may lead to moisture entering the mobile home and problems/mold in the wall cavities.

Tip: Push hard on every exterior wall when walking through a potential mobile home investment. The wall should be very sturdy and not feel loose due to wood rot.

Amateur Electric

It is common for mobile homeowners to make their own electrical repairs over the years. You may see electrical outlets that do not work, extension cords running across the home, wires hanging from ceiling electrical outlets, and other obviously "amateur-style" repair jobs.

Tip: Remember that it is often wise to hire a professional electrician when dealing with repairs.

Questionable Plumbing

Is common for mobile homeowners to make their own plumbing repairs over time. If you are unsure of any plumbing issues, always consult a professional.

Tip: Before purchasing any investment property, make sure to check that the hot water heater works, that all plumbing seems to work, that there is no evidence of leaks inside or out, etc.

Ceiling Repairs

It is common for many mobile homeowners to make their own repairs over the years. When it comes to roof and ceiling repairs, many homeowners may not do things 100 percent correctly. Over time, these mistakes and oversights may allow moisture/water to seep into the roof, causing additional problems, wood rot, mildew and mold to develop over time.

Tip: Before purchasing any investment property, make sure to understand all repairs needed in the home. Also, ask sellers how they made certain repairs and feel free to raise/unscrew ceiling panels to look and feel around in the ceiling to ensure you know exactly what you are buying.

Doors Missing

It is common for interior mobile home doors to go missing. These may be ordered at specialty mobile home supply stores locally or over the Internet at mobile home-related websites.

Holes in Walls

It is common for the interior of some older mobile homes to have holes in the walls. While these repairs are cosmetic, they can certainly go a long way in helping you resell the home.

Tip: Replacing broken wall panels and/or fixing drywall can be a quick "test repair job" for a new handyman you may be trying out. Give prospective handyman a small area of wall to fix. After the job is complete, you can review the speed and quality of each person to choose whom you will continue using. Always keep on the lookout for more experienced mobile home handymen.

More Than One Source of Air Conditioning

Be aware when a homeowner has multiple cooling systems for their home. Swamp coolers, window AC units, central HVAC systems, fans, etc. all serve the purpose to cool down a home's interior temperature. Make sure you know which systems work and which do not. If a seller has more than one source of air conditioning, then it is highly likely that one of these systems does not work properly.

Tip: Unless you are able to verify repairs needed, do not simply trust/believe what a seller tells you about a non-functional appliance. If you cannot physically test this appliance or system, then you must assume it is broken and will need a good deal of money to be replaced or fixed.

Missing Insulation

Always check underneath every mobile home to verify a majority of the insulation is still intact underneath the home. This layer of thick insulation should be supported by a vapor barrier/water barrier to keep out moisture. This vapor barrier may be a dark blue or black color and should stretch along the entire underside of the manufactured home.

CHAPTER 12
SPECIFIC WORDS MOBILE HOME INVESTORS SHOULD KNOW

As an active real estate investor and/or mobile home investor, it is important to know common words and terminology used on a daily basis. This article will cover the lesser-known words that may only come up sporadically while investing in manufactured housing.

Toter

This is the uniquely designed truck used for transporting, towing, and sometimes re-leveling a new or used mobile home. This specially designed truck often has the capacity to use hydraulics to lift and maneuver a mobile home into its final exact destination quickly and easily. This piece of equipment is typically owned by your local mobile home transport companies.

Tongue

A mobile home is typically pulled down the highway by its tongue. A mobile home's "tongue" is the V-shaped metal piece on the front of the mobile home that allows it to be pulled by a truck. There are two types of tongues. The first is welded on and is permanent. The second is bolted on and only installed when moving the home. As used mobile home investors, we oftentimes do not have the ability to pick and choose which type of tongue our mobile homes have. Either type of tongue will be satisfactory if the mobile home needs to be moved.

Tip: Concerning welded-on tongues, look for any broken weld or rust that might suggest that the tongue cannot pull the home safely. Concerning bolted-on tongues, make sure the tongue is present and accounted for (it's usually found under the home for safe storage).

Roof Flashing

Roof flashing is the metal strip that keeps exterior water from coming in between the roof and the walls (including the ventilation pipes in the roof) and where they meet. Almost all mobile home roof flashing is a thin gauge sheet metal held to the roof with a sticky sealant.

Damaged roof flashing will allow water to permeate inside the exterior walls of the home. After months and years of continual wetness within a mobile home wall, there may likely be serious mold and/or wood rot developing and destroying the wall from within.

Tip: Roof flashing can be a very complicated thing to fix. You will know this by the persistence of roof leaks after you have attempted to fix the damaged flashing. Before you begin to work on any roof, make sure you are competent in the repairs or are using an experienced professional to help solve the problem. Identify the problem and remove and replace the damaged materials.

Heat Tape

Heat tape is the technology that keeps the water lines from freezing and bursting during freezing weather. Heat tape wraps exterior/interior water lines and normally runs throughout a mobile home.

There are typically two types of heat tape used in mobile homes. Both are fairly similar. The first type looks like an average extension cord that is wrapped around water pipes to keep them above the freezing temperature point. The second type of heat tape found is a silver coil that is cut to fit the water line and attach to a plug at one end. From personal experience, this second type typically lasts longer.

Vapor Barrier

A mobile home's vapor barrier is a black plastic mesh material located under the insulation under the mobile home. The vapor barrier usually spans the mobile home from end to end and from side to side. A mobile home's vapor barrier has a few main purposes. This material helps to keep your utility bills low, plus it adds protection to your plumbing to help keep pipes from freezing in colder states. This vapor barrier also assists the insulation in helping to keep harmful vapors from entering into the living areas of the mobile home.

Tip: Your mobile home's vapor barrier material should not be torn or missing. You will see this underneath your investment mobile home. A sagging vapor barrier could be a sign of water leaks and moister damage. Simply remove and replace any damaged material underneath the home. Vapor barriers can be installed and secured with a simple heavy-duty staple gun.

In conclusion, mobile homes are more similar than they are different. Many of the same terms and phrases used in traditional homebuilding will be used for factory built homes as well. In the future, if you ever have a question about a certain word or the unclear meaning of any terminology, never hesitate to speak up and ask for clarity. Clarity is the only way to invest with knowledge and safety, so make sure to get your questions answered promptly. Continue investing and reaching out to help local sellers daily.

CHAPTER 13
BENEFITS OF A MOBILE HOME PARK INVESTMENT

Let's face it: When people think of mobile homes they conjure up the most stereotypical images of run-down trailer parks with a substandard way of life. While there are definitely certain mobile home parks, which uphold this stereotype, there are many more, which offer a peaceful and aesthetically pleasing lifestyle. What people fail to consider about mobile home parks is that the owner of each park is raking in thousands of dollars a month on lot rent alone.

Quick and Reliable ROI

Whether you have the capital to invest yourself or you, need to acquire a mortgage to purchase land or an already operational mobile home park, your net income will sufficiently reimburse you and/or cover the mortgage with profit left over. The more lots that are available to accommodate mobile homes, the higher your monthly revenue becomes. If you are renting out lots and collecting rent on mobile homes, your monthly gross income could easily be in the tens of thousands of dollars. Even if you're only renting out lots to those who own their own trailers, you could still make that much money in a month, depending on how many lots your land contains. With income in these numbers, you will be able to pay a significant amount towards the principal of your mortgage loan to save a couple bucks in interest while shaving years off the life of your loan.

Finding an Investment Opportunity

While investing in mobile home parks can be quite lucrative, actually getting into the market can prove to be quite challenging. You may be lucky enough to find a mobile home park that is up for sale; but generally speaking, you have a ton of homework and research to conduct in order to find a good opportunity. Basically, you have 2 options: Purchase an already operational mobile home park or purchase land and however many trailers you can afford to put on the land.

If you choose to create a mobile home park out of nothing, make sure you have the capital to support such a project. Not only will you need sufficient capital, you must adhere to all local zoning laws. Remember that you will need to add plumbing and electricity to the land itself before it can be hooked up to mobile homes. Before you decide to build your own mobile home park, make sure to perform all due diligence not only to find out through which proverbial hoops you'll have to jump, but also to make sure you have the budget to see the entire project through. To get your new mobile homes selling or renting as quickly as possible, offer move in specials for renters and owner financing for the trailers themselves.

If you are interested in finding a park, which is already operational, you may have your best luck in seeking out privately owned mobile home parks, often referred to as "Ma and Pa Lots." These types of trailer parks account for roughly 35% of all mobile home parks in the US, and many of them are not as profitable as they could be. It's possible that owners of these types of parks could be bought out for the right price.

Once you've done all your homework and have found the best mobile home park investment opportunity, here are a few ways to make sure your investment stays profitable.

Keep Rent in Line with Inflation

Every year, the cost of living increases. There are many factors at play when it comes time to determine the cost of lot rent. While you want to offer fair and affordable prices, you also need to reap a sufficient enough profit to justify your investment. Re-assess your P&L documentation at least quarterly to ensure your prices are amply covering costs and you are reaching your target profit margin.

Short Leases or Month to Month Rentals

The best way to keep yourself protected from limitation on rent is to only engage in short term leases or rent only on a month-to-month basis. It's difficult to anticipate every cost which may arise – especially if you are a landlord of rented mobile homes on your land. Your budget could change in an instant, and you should have the flexibility of increasing rent with proper notice.

Consider the Cost of Utilities

If you plan to cover the expenses of some or all utilities, take your overall cost and divide it by the number of lots you're actively renting on a monthly basis – especially if you have multiple changes in residency. Review this information regularly to ensure that the costs of the utilities you offer are not cutting too deeply into your net profit.

CONCLUSION

Mobile home parks might not be viewed as such an attractive investment to add to your portfolio at first glance, but when you look into the consistency of tenancies and the income you can generate, they can potentially be an attractive real estate investment.

Many low-income tenants actively seek out mobile homes to live in as opposed to low rent apartments, as it gives them privacy and a better quality of life. This means they are often more than happy to stay where they are, especially when you consider the prohibitive moving costs of transporting a mobile home.

The end result is a mobile home park full of tenants who can provide you with a stable rental income, so it may well be worth investigating some sites that are available to acquire from existing owners, as an alternative investment that could potentially deliver some solid returns.

ABOUT THE AUTHOR

When my real estate career began in 2002, I, like so many others, approached it with all the excitement and passion, a can-do attitude. Within eight months, I was all but out of a real estate career until one day when a profound game-changing experience would be revealed, and my real estate career would instantly transform.

Before entering real estate, I was in another profession as I acquired my real estate license in mid-2002. In my prior field of work, I had the honor to be among the top in the insurance industry and thought immediately upon entering the real estate profession I made the naïve assumption I would be an instant SUCCESS. Keep in mind; I was not aware of the actual mechanics of success, let alone in a position to speak about success. At the time, it was an unknown illusion for me. All that was going for me in my favor was an unconscious misunderstanding of the "Burning Desire" to succeed.

When saying I attempted everything back in 2002, that would be an understatement. Even as late as writing the book: Art of the Open House, in 2018,

I still was no closer to understanding the much-needed revelation behind it all.

The most essential component that I had failed to see during this time was the Mind Power needed to make the difference. Without understanding the power of the subconscious mind, all attempts to grasp hold of success will fade into the sunset. A person's destiny cannot be seen if the mind is stuck in the past, learn from the past, live in the present, and create a new future.

The thoughts you think, that you will become.

If you think you are a success, a success you will be.

BOOKS AVAILABLE:

- Art of the Open House
- Secretos de Éxito de Bienes Raíces *(Spanish Edition)*
- Eyes of a Real Estate Professional
- Mind Power to Real Estate

www.ingramcontent.com/pod-product-compliance
Lightning Source LLC
Chambersburg PA
CBHW030705220526
45463CB00005B/1912